MW00582769

Eveningful

Copyright 2024 by Jennifer Whalen

All rights reserved

Printed in the United States of America

Cover art by Jennifer Whalen using imagery sampled from *New Theory of Colors* (1808) by Mary Gartside. These images were also sampled throughout this book.

Cover and interior layout by Jem Ashton

This book is set in Athelas and Rig Sans

Lightscatter Press is an independent nonprofit literary press with 501(c)(3) tax-exempt status that seeks to preserve and extend the material, tactile experience of the printed, bound text through beautiful, innovative design that integrates digital artifacts and experiences created for and with the printed text. Our home is Salt Lake City, Utah.

Library of Congress Control Number: 2024932028
Names: Whalen, Jennifer, Author
Title: Eveningful, Poems by Jennifer Whalen
Description: Salt Lake City, Lightscatter Press (2024)
Identifiers: Library of Congress Contol Number: 2024932028
                  ISBN: 978-1-7364835-4-1
                  (trade paperback)

First printing

Lightscatter Press
Salt Lake City, Utah
www.lightscatterpress.org

Eveningful

Poems

Jennifer Whalen

LIGHTSCATTER
PRESS

Contents

Late-medieval Books of Hours were, among other things, tools for meditating on and regulating intimate time. In a contemporary interpretation of this practice, *Eveningful* has a virtual Book of Time, to reflect the book's deliberation on the power of various thresholds to regulate and free the self. With your phone camera, scan the QR codes you encounter within this printed book, and you will be taken to the virtual Book of Time, where you will find vivid details from artist Elizabeth Fuller's paintings, as well as audio recordings of the poet reading the poems.

Foreword by Rick Barot

Manhattan, early morning. Incongruously, a whip-poor-will is sounding its wake-up call in one of the courtyard's trees. Caught in a tree's branches just outside the fourth-floor window, two deflated mylar balloons sway in the spring breeze. It had been a late night. In the velvety dimness of a club, we listened to a jazz quartet, followed by an aimless walking-around in the chilly streets. We watched people slip into their buildings, people clustered outside places waiting to be allowed in, and people walking in the hurried directions of their desires.

Because of the pandemic, because I had not been in the city for years, the poetry of cities kept rushing to mind. T.S. Eliot, of course: "Let us go then, you and I, / When the evening is spread out against the sky / Like a patient etherized upon a table." And this quick glimpse from Eileen Myles: "A woman / chewing gum by the window / of the train. Which heaves / its accordion on & we move." And then, because I had been in the atmosphere of Jennifer Whalen's *Eveningful* for weeks, I remembered the vibe of these lines from "The World Wants":

> The world won't tell me
> what it wants, but I think it likes when stepping
> from my car door, I quickly flash the pink
> of my underwear. It did this undulation
> in the leaves. It doesn't need party hat invitations.
> I think I owe the world a thank you.
> It didn't ask me to come here,
> to sit at this bar top & buy myself a drink,
> & yet I still came.

That flash of pink. In Whalen's poems, disclosures are made the way you would tell a closely held story about yourself to a stranger at a party. The disclosures are like charms, part of the bright, brief scene. The energy of festivity infuses the poems. As in the first lines of "The Gold Door," the book's first poem: "When I enter a gold door, I want to enter / a gold door." And a couple of beats later, to be even clearer about it: "I mean that upon entering / the door, something grand / should be waiting." An eager expectancy is a principal mood in Whalen's poems, harbored in speakers who have a gorgeous and witty urbanity:

> We want the world to reveal
>
> its magic more often than not: the crowd bursts
>
> into song—you don't know
>
> if it's pen ink or blueberry juice
>
> on your hands. The moon dips into the river
>
> as if to cleanse its plump body...

But wanting the world is one thing, and having it is another. Because even though a kind of gusto defines the sensibility of Whalen's poems, they are also defined by the ennui and melancholy of their cosmopolitanism. "Party Planning," announces the title of one poem— only to meet the later sentiment of another poem's title, "The Heart That Loves Is Always Wrong." Like no other vision I have encountered recently, Whalen in her poetry paints the textures of modern city life, its abstract and concrete qualities, its gloss and grit.

Ardor is an arduous thing in Whalen's world, perhaps because something like its opposite—solitude, or simply being one's self—has a preferable seduction. A surge within the self for connection is always alongside the wish for a knowing aloneness. As the speaker in "A Light" declares: "My lonely / will never know a lonely quite like its own." And later, observing a moth inside the house, the speaker says, with witty melancholy: "Look how flighty / & close it is. It thinks / I am a light." The tension between that flightiness and that closeness is what gives Whalen's poems their pathos. Especially when that tension is deep in the self, as exquisitely formulated in "On Appeal":

Not every room has a window seat.

Eyes need light if the iris color is to catch.

Whatever work remains after decoration, is ours.

Some days love is light with fluff

& easy. She either wears the red shoes

or she won't.

Poised between Eliot's love song and Myles's snapshot, Whalen's poems have an aching passion. Like the whip-poor-will and balloons of the morning after, they keep dazzling me back into an alertness towards my own intimate life. *Eveningful* is about elation and sorrow and the way they can happen almost at the same time, together. The poems are about an avid delight, yes: "Like sleeping / in someone's favorite sweater, waking up / with its fine threads in my mouth." And also yes: "Sometimes the rain / has to start, then stop. Your life will be full / of something; that will have to be enough." Among the poems in *Eveningful* are three titled

"It's Seven," "It's Nine," and "It's Twelve." Which is to say, the evening is always getting later and deeper, like the heart or like adulthood, arriving at the other side of the night as always:

> I wanted morning to be bright:
> a few puddles the sun hadn't scorched out,
> grass greener, vines vinier,
> the day swollen with plump & me,
> necessary form among forms:
> the rivulets of a skirt made more lovely with wind's wavering.
> But it was just morning.
> Long dry clear singing morning.

I

The Gold Door

When I enter a gold door, I want to enter
a gold door. Consider how a drawer
only responds to specific tracks
to align its wheels. I mean that upon entering
the door, something grand
should be waiting. I ask for small things
of the array of things one can ask for:
I ask nothing of the goldness
of the door, that it sparkle in certain light
or lack flakes revealing
its initial finish. I ask nothing
of how long I should be allowed inside
or in what manner I must interact,
as in when I enter a room of strangers,
I ask to be greeted in a manner fitting
to my entering. I will bring a bottle with a bow
& exit empty handed. These are expectations
ingrained in the fabric of evenings,
as in when I enter a room of oranges,
I wish to be wrapped in silk satin
& remembered with such shimmer
in times of trouble. To hold this thought
is to meet on most necessary terms,
like letting the moon stand as a symbol of night
& therefore be less of night. The grand thing
can be wrapped in a box or framed
in the mind or written in lily-water. It can be

grand in that it is largesse or grand
in that it is precise. It can greet me by name
or be present in the palm. It can be orange
in color or warped in form. When I enter
 a gold door, I want to be equal
with what I meet & then you will know
I have asked nothing of you.

Party Planning

What about the confetti? Somebody
would have to pick it out, another
clean it up. I wasn't a mathematician;
I wouldn't add up the parts to some whole.
Even if I did, how romantic could it be?
a roll of streamer paper cut to slivers
under a factory laser—but still,
I had a choice & like any choice,
I stalled. Bathroom breaks, trips
to snack machines, watching tiny spirals
nudge chocolate towards connoisseurs,
but what about the confetti?
If I paced party stores—bagged paper-shapes,
scrapped rainbow crumbs—what then?
would one reach to me as if a bare hand
towards the heat? I tried to visualize
the world through bits
of paper: the gas station ground
covered in color, street corners
camouflaged in faux-petals swept
to mountains later. It was ridiculous,
all of it, night's accentuated cause
& effect: our throwing
then cheering. But I would have to live
within it, hair speckled in evening-excess,
or seconds prior: when confetti
is just confetti, not a mirror to hold

the night to. Could anyone have turned on me
for lack of effort? If I returned empty-handed
or wrong-handed or not at all. Confetti:
a word in my mouth, the night now rid
of its taskliness. And if they did turn,
offered faces as masks of grimace,
little clamors of *it was never meant to be*,
wouldn't this blame be an effort,
a perfectly arranged bouquet,
a mirror to see the night through?

Even in Disguise

I.

Talk leans small over the balcony rails:
is this starlight member to some far-off nebula?
Tell me the longevity of any given swan.
I didn't belong there. Not that I didn't love
swans & stars & parties, I did; I do.
On twitchy summer days, I think *there is a sun*;
I could do something worthwhile
with my hands: gum wrappers born new
as tiny creased birds; party gifts to strangers
on streets. But this night was different
than that wanting. I wanted to fall in love
with a daffodil for its daffodilness; not
those fundamental facets that make it unlike
a daisy. Others thought this wishy-
washy, neither here nor there. Like an unfolded
then refolded paperclip, I was neither my former
love nor this newer, loppy self. But this
was a dinner party!—love was both in
& out of the question.

2.

When I plead to the bus
not to crash its broad side into mine,
I mean there are countless avenues. Impact
is merely one. I could forgive a frog its lonely
croaking, teach a sponge-scrub the inside corners
of an oven. It is better to believe
our nebulae into some good warning: the stuff
in the sky that makes dancing-nights
worth dancing; someone in our midst
who comes to learn my recipes, who longs
to love my loves.

If I Erase My Body

I'll start with the cunt
because I like a real-deal
roll-up-your-sleeves kind of challenge
because the middle is as good a place
as any because the thought of that being the only-me
reminds me of every electric socket
I've tried to crawl into because
it would be like washing the sheets
after sorry sex or scrubbing my name
from the band of my underwear
because I like the thought of it folding
into a hundred-sided polygon & harrowing
into my heart because I'm tired of carrying it
light as a locket but heavy as the faded mother
within because sometimes I imagine it soft
as a small chipmunk nuzzling my ankle whimpering
for milk because it's aloof & confuses
whose tongue-ridge is worth remembering
because it doesn't respond to its own name
in my mouth because it can't decide how gingerly
you should collect its petals because
it wants to exist finally free
of description because the windowsills
dangle wasp nests & there's already too many hollows
to decorate my worry because if gone

it couldn't be gotten to because
if this is my erasing, I choose
where it starts.

A Cantaloupe

I bought a cantaloupe, left it round
on the counter—a small sign, offered
nourishment. It didn't transform
into carriages. I stayed the same
in wonderment: four nights, then five,
silent. Some wise women claim the fruit
of the earth is always in the palm
of the hand. I've never tasted
a cantaloupe, unsure of what dish
to make. It's warm in the room
where I contemplate past love.
How pleasant it seems with slight sweat
on skin. How round is the cantaloupe,
how unlike flowers or scented branches.
Potpourri, small candles—can I fragrant
a place into a home? I bought
a cantaloupe, cut it down to small slices
like dismembering a chair or remembering
a dead friend. How quickly
I eradicated these things from me, upset
I couldn't swallow them whole.

Eleven Versions of Taking Off My Lover

1.

Silk smooths the jut-blades
of my shoulders, rushes
the quick slope of my arms.
A robe-puddle pools the floor.
Nothing hangs from me.

2.

Some houses have secret upstairs,
secret basements,
lofts no one knows of,
underground bombing huddles.
Sometimes you realize your lover
is not your lover.
This is funny architecture.

3.

Mistaken sight is perhaps best sight.
A stack of coffee filters resembling
a giant seashell. The image only disintegrates
when I try to approach it.
Stupid desire; careful lover.

4.

I'm taking off my lover
today
like eliminating lactose
or calling my landlord.
There is no getting around it.

5.

Do lovers speak in absolutes to know language
at its most vulnerable
when it falls through? Do they like
the sound of words shifting air? Is it dainty
like powdering your nose
or heavy like the hard setting
on your shower head?

6.

Broken watch, torn seam.
Every lover has the same dream
I'm certain: things right themselves
when we're not looking.

7.

First, you notice one long black hair
on your pillow, then two,
then it's on your shoulder;
half your day is picking hairs
from your place, your person.
And when your lover is not
your lover, you find solace
in spoiled metaphors: how hair
is dead—how its beauty is dependent
on its deadness. How each new inch
is just an extension of ending.
And you're not happy with this sham-symbol
you've latched, but it's simple,
& now it's latched.

8.

First find the color to match the button.
Then imagine your hands as tiny knot-renders.
You are a little fixer
of things, you are the threader of needles,
restitcher of buttons; the thread is a wet ripple
in your mouth. Look at me,
look how simple
this trick is. Are you watching?
Watch.

9.

My favorite stars are the ones I find suddenly
& without effort that strike me
as somehow bold in their stealth.
And when I can't place them the next night,
I forget their secrecy is what beamed
my love in the first place. Then
it's like I never had a lover.

10.

Sometimes I imagine my lover
taking me off. Was it a fabric swatch a day?
Or fast & swift: all singular pronouns
& past tense? I wonder if my lovers ever
put me back on. Like lingerie bought
to entice whatever self waits in the mirror.
I wonder if they wake from some dream & lie
in the clumsy rivers of their sheets sifting
my idea. Do they rise & grind
coffee grounds until that sound
is the only sound to start their day?
I wonder if my lovers still see me
in cream shapes in their mugs.
I wonder what they would do
if I appeared before them,
if I put myself back on.

II.

Sometimes I don't take off my lover
at all—just cover & coat & put on.
A woman's portrait gazes
beneath patches of grass
only electromagnetic energy
can ungrow. In this metaphor,
I'm not the canvas. In this metaphor,
I'm not even the painter. Maybe
I'm just the viewer who happens
on that final layer, that wild-secret patch,
& loves it.

Interior Music

The train's sad siren seemed to move distances,
up rocky peaks & through trees
harboring water in their roots, to reach us.

We imagined the faraway train rolling
perpetually farther away
but slowly. Whatever destination it slinked towards,

it wouldn't reach by morning. Then, the cricket
in the yard. First, one, its voice,
a steady tapping; then two, friends

or mates; then hundreds,
all applause. We knew our neighbors:
their coarse yells,

but how much love they housed
in their throats, we couldn't say.
Inside, the refrigerator barreled through ice.

Each cube clanked hard against the pile,
a self-made monument to cold. Next,
the candle's wick muttered

slightest crackling, as if burning
should be soothing. Finally, the only noises
left to notice were human: a maneuver

in the stomach, a long wrought exhale,
a shift in position or mood.
What if the mind's interior made such music?

Not sounds of memory, murky
& dependent upon conjuring,
but thought-squeaks, blasts, feedback,

how our bodies push against something,
& there is a whole range of response—
like opening a door: the familiar creak

of hinges, then whistles & engines,
winds & waters, cars & their drivers:
the outside rushing in.

The Heart That Loves Is Always Wrong

I want to see the world: pure setting without context.

Flower buds not in the image of Spring,
but blooms in & of
themselves.

As if waking having never slept;
as if sleeping with no hope of dreaming.

I want to be singular as if spurred from nothing.

The wind is having its time with the maple leaves.
Pretty soon, it'll be bare.

A gas station pump free
of all my ideas of gas station pumps.
I want to press its buttons like a crisp language.

Inside my heart is another heart, but smaller
& more aware of itself.
There isn't a place in the state where I could meet you
as you are.

The wind is having its time with the window screen:
a looseness that won't wobble out.

I want to turn to you as if breaking fresh from molding.

The one heart is just as wrong as the other.
They can't seem to love a thing right.

II

It's Seven

So like the delicate setting
of a picnic blanket in the sun,
the bright dining room hushed

to a dim-lit corridor.
Patrons slid off their heels, smeared bare feet
against legs beneath tablecloths.

I don't know why our sex breathes
in shadows. Yes, exceptions abound.
Somewhere there's a meadow

where people love in the sun,
maybe. But that room had robbed time
of time—strange, I know,

but I needed the sunset-splayed
brawny yawn across day; the sun
sliding down, slow-down,

until it halos some hill. I tried
to pretend love waited in this—forking
an Alaskan fish, my eyes just shy

of refusing eye contact.
It is too much to have a body,
to monitor its functions

so on luck-lustered nights
it meets another body—a toast!
to pat fork against glass

while expanding my throat:
I had this grand feeling something
grand should happen, but

the waiter waltzed round
lighting candles as if silent ceremony
followed next. The evening kept on

flickering shoddy evening
when I imagined myself moving—
faint figure on a dense floor

drifting deeply to melody,
sweat-peppered skin; how glorious we
can be when only vague fractions.

If I leave now, go
west away enough, it may still be dark
when I get there.

The Party

We strung light bulbs from tree branches;
our bodies were still bodies,
but they couldn't make brightness
for us—not with the itch of pollen
in the air, our noses all sneezes
& sniffling. I liked autumn in that
I liked cardigans hung rickety
from people's shoulders; the night
would be lovely because we knew
our role in rendering it so.
I was the thing I usually am,
like the stagehand whose sole job
is to pull curtain ropes on cue,
I feigned necessary tasks (punch to taste,
banners to hang) then finally
said hello. Most didn't see their place
in the scheme, but with what grace they had,
they played. Some would remember
the evening, but as shards: warm glow
in the leaves, a small fire
by an open door. In retrospect,
I wanted to keep the heat lamps
& tenderness out of it. I imagined
this occasion my creation
since I thought to sweep light
through trees. But maybe it was the person
who picked the music or the woman

who clicked the scene to pictures,
a ravenous flicker in our midst.
We were trying to make something
where something already stood: our night
layered on the darkness & stars
that made night possible regardless
of our loving it so. It would permeate
past the pollen-soaked air,
bright bulbs gleaming through green
or no. Still, I'd be lying
if I said you could have been anyone,
that it was the night I really loved.

Singing

I.

It would keep raining; this I knew.
Steady rain: tinny drops pattering the car top.
No thunder boom, rhythm to fall drowsy in.
The sky, slate gray: it would take days to pour out.
So I laced boots up my ankles,
coat zipped to my neck; I would get wet.

Reflection all around: stop lights on water falling,
street bulbs in puddles.
The road, a damp dark cool, but such light!
When I knew no one would turn to me,
ask *what's stirring high up in that head of yours*,
I loved the puddles' red-blue blinking OPEN
more than the signs themselves.
Tell me there are worse digressions.

2.

The rain would end; this I grew
to value. Like a four-leaf clover in a sea of three,
we must trust the world to shape landscapes
where luck can give way. Still,
it takes a particular labor to love a thing as it ends.
The best to hope for was rain to trickle out slow
in the night, wake with blunt light
bleating through blinds.

I wanted morning to be bright:
a few puddles the sun hadn't scorched out,
grass greener, vines vinier,
the day swollen with plump & me,
necessary form among forms:
the rivulets of a skirt made more lovely with wind's wavering.
But it was just morning.
Long dry clear singing morning.

We Want the World

I tire of people who leave

crosswords half-whole, stuck
on some word they never entered the right room
in the right lighting to learn

the meaning of. Is there a prize
for basic diligence? Will I find it
in a supercenter before

the sun wanders the horizon?
I only came here to replace a blow dryer
that howled so loud it blew out.

We want the world to reveal
its magic more often than not: the crowd bursts
into song—you don't know

if it's pen ink or blueberry juice
on your hands. The moon dips into the river
as if to cleanse its plump body,

glistering the water yellow.
I imagine myself a lesser messenger
assigned to data retrieval,

some cog in the larger structure.
The curator of menial tasks who watches
lovers, keeps tally of whose eyes

close first when they kiss.

To Better Describe It

The night—shameless thing brightened
by breaking plates & dying
candles—came less like a thief
& more like a grief counselor
on a TV set where an actress
recently passed. Not that
it was a distinctly somber
evening or callous morning.
Not that it wished to be reversed,
but longed to be remembered
at its most endearing.

A clank of a glass scurried
all useless noises away.
I forgot the sound of running
water, pages turning, creasing
into companions. The smell
was the crisp after-rain,
but it hadn't rained in weeks.
Not that I was crazy,
but the night had smoothed itself
in such a way the impossible
was possible again.

When I realized the effortlessness
it would take to extend
this new feeling, I started touching:

first, the bar top, sticky,
then smooth. Next, curtains laced
inside windows. Then I moved
to crowd-people, twirling inwards,
then out. My limbs turned airy
to compact into so many memories;
I still search for words to better describe it.

When asked, I invented professions,
becoming a person
who tests hard, gelatin candies, sucking
until my lips turn cherry red,
then berry blue. The night's refrain
now a nascence of proof:
a spun-out dance
where it is easy to lie when surely
there was a time I could have been anything,
but I ended up as this.

What Will Devastate

My heart stops, my body
becomes its own catacomb, I find myself
ten years older having never found
that red windbreaker.

                     I think a hand brushes
my shoulder, but it's just a rib
of an umbrella.

              A hoarse voice
hovers a plainly plucked guitar.

Shattered teacup
              inert on the kitchen tile.

My fingertips scrupulously trace
each swollen
              hair follicle, each crooked
freckle. My eyes cannot see my body
close enough.

              My heart becomes its own anchor,
my body, the deep ditch I will live
to dig up through.

              What will devastate arrives
through phone wires, blood draws:
sometimes my lovers cry
when they call.

              Near dusk,

final stitch.
            What will devastate
pools puddles
            on the floor where I undress,
the pillow my head slept.
What will devastate
                hasn't devastated yet.

The World Will Not Meet You Here

where weeds bend from walkways
& wind teases the fabric from your legs,
but you can always turn to the world.
Waiting for the sun to lower or a feeling
to hold, you perfected patience
to stillness—was this not what you wanted?
Huddled in an overcoat, wisps still wander
through walls where you are;
there is no covering grand enough.
Some nights feel as worlds
without effort: they arrive as if rewards
for clinging so diligently to your memory.
Words were wrung out on you
but never in sounds stern enough,
so they pierced your guilt but never your reason.
You cannot think a route back to devotion.
Here, somewhere, dried rose petals
scattered to remind that crisping a surface
reveals so little of within. The world
will not meet you here where the music chooses
itself & there is always some silver new
& shiny to tarnish. You were right to be weary
of loving so rickety & without outcome
that the self drains thin—but dearling,
shouldn't the world just once
fill you with fever enough
to fire? Wisdom will not greet you here

where the stairs have railings
& the rooms no balconies to fall.
Caution will take you somewhere safe
& in that bathhouse of vigilance, this streetcar
of exceptional direction, time is too wide
to marvel; the days, too long to stay.

The Beginning

What taught me worry? Who twirled
dark gauze over my eyes?
Who mapped my body, made
these aches a scrawled key?
On the drive home, I pass a forest
crisp & pale & leafless from flame.
My task is to loose myself
from this image, to feel empty distinctly
for the trees. What mantra will leave me,
clean me—what sunset, what water,
what ode? Who taught me worry?
What pattern stitched so sturdy
I can't unravel? Who will clasp me,
coat me, care me—who will fuck me
threadless? What stick did I pick up
that won't stuck down? What luck
latched that won't clash out? Sometimes
I wake & the day is its own introduction:
the gold blades searing the floor are the sun;
if you feel dizzy, drink warm milk;
you're in your bed, this blank-trauma
is in your head; if your head's spinning,
here's some honey; remember
your body weaves miracles,
you could have a baby. If you're dizzy,

remember the world is spinning.
Who taught you worry? Lay down,
speak steady, start from the beginning.

The Expansion

Once we were content to be children.
Then, even feathered seedheads
of the tallest grasses couldn't cover
us. Our limbs grew strange

in their bodies; we became our own
feathered covering. Like grasshoppers,
we felt an oncoming in our wings:
the dewy wet before drizzle

in our hair. Indoors, we twirled to see
our backs in the mirror. Bare & smooth,
it took a quiet getting used to.
We grew to recognize the world

in its reactions against us. When our shoes
clogged to waterlog, we could point
to rain. When dry & stiffly,
we couldn't. This was the loosest,

least dear, of any knowing.
The weight of fingers sifting
piano keys, wind railing
hard against a building—we felt

our possible lives siphoning
then evaporating. Few words rang
for such precise gnawing.
Bluebonnets sprang the skirts

of interstates. We wanted to be
beautiful without incident,
long-low willow leaves brushing
a pond unseen. But the sky,

it hid its forecast, dividing clouds
into fluff polka dots. And our thoughts,
they couldn't be stopped: old fields, starch stems
gliding our sides, our palms' soft center.

It would take such an intricate
unravel to climb back in. We weren't older
than the sky we swayed under,
but we were as old as we'd ever been.

On Patience

Surely, it is some keen grace that leads:
craving turned resting turned null.

A doorbell's ring took field lengths to address.
Who could say who rang & who answered?

As if stillness formed longing,
then resolved, the piano plays itself.

We made pockets, placid & proportionate.
Distances later, we found each other older & secure.

III

It's Nine

I am always elsewhere even
when here. Like the procession of a band
of drummers, sticks rapping snares,

we run roads to our rightful
setting. Not that where we happened
before wasn't formal or true,

but how tempting to think
our new aim is the proper place to be.
Is it unfair to take shape?

if half the size, think how many
people could swarm this room, breathe this perfume.
Bodies enchant other bodies;

so little to lament
without: no tardiness, no gluttony—
will the clock ever chime nine

& I sink darkly into
& not through? Someone's groping the ground
for car keys; someone's fallen

rich & full in love
with a piano's frequencies.
Their spectacle, a gift

we, the stationary, get to see.
I want to admire this anatomy
for its feeling, not its reason—

these arms, our legs' memory
of billows to carry beat. Most beings
don't need records of evening

to keep on being: trees
tussling their leaves, nuzzling high atop
the heat, their bodies rocking

their heads—I can listen.

Place Shape

Darkness hazed the nightclub's bathroom:
women smearing liner into coves
of their eyes, every stall door painted black.

Someone ripped the mural of Jackie Kennedy;
I didn't recognize these people
or the thoughts they made me feel.

With my eyes on my eyes in the mirror,
I fumbled essentialism:
I didn't want Whitman to be wrong—yes,

yes we have our multitudes,
but in that particular moment I thought
of the various shapes I take, this shape

is something like the realest. Hours later,
I tried to fathom Jackie as past tense,
reeling rooms as if to track an exact path

to the dance floor would slip me
closer to purity. Not purity
like white sheets & chastity

but purity like symphonies
dwindling down to the sound
of a single set of strings.

I wanted a song I could mouth words through.
I pretended invisibility. Even in reduced form,
I couldn't fold inward slim enough.

Both the spectated & spectator,
I was too timid to look right alone.
Maybe I was just being hard on myself.

I've never worked up the resolve
to start clawing walls. Once I stole a candle
from a table to keep a single evening

near me. But to fling to a hard surface
stripping layers of Jackie's face,
who takes that form?

She's somewhere on that floor,
but not a shape I'll take. Soon,
I missed weather, moved through

a backdoor: the breeze in the night,
the night rippling folds in my clothes.
There's a lesson somewhere in here,

but I can't pan high enough to see it
or zoom near enough to live it.
A man sat near me on a stone wedge.

I didn't take his cigarette. He's not a light
to carry with me. He asked what song
I'd like to bear. Maybe the night's solace

is every shape has a chance
to change; it's the everpressure
of possibility that rings the same.

On Appeal

Not every room has a window seat.
Eyes need light if the iris color is to catch.
Whatever work remains after decoration, is ours.

Some days love is light with fluff
& easy. She either wears the red shoes
or she won't.

Portrait on a Train to the City

A hand blends the soft
    edges of my calf
the way work crews clean the aftermath
of car crashes,
      sweeping glass
to the edges of grass.

I've traveled long enough,
    far enough,
that I welcome the observer
(the scribbling pencil, the half-worn eraser),
who can only guess
      what tired images
crowd my walls.

There was a time a hand touched me
& I became a gift unwrapping itself,
    & then, again,
although I could never learn
to return
      to the spring.

I find an allure in this
(train rides, infatuation,
    the blending stump),
in its already half-dead inscription.

I feel the charcoal
        simultaneously
enter & exit my skin
as suspense, the draft from an open
train door,
a hand outside my leg.

The World Wants

The world is too much tonight:
too much vibration, vibrato.
The breeze is doing too much
with the trees, the flag, the tablecloth, the grass.
The sunset is loud & alarming; it is an overheard
conversation about addiction. I am listening.
I say *slow down*. I say *waft loose*.
I sit stern with my hands clasped in my lap
so I am not another moving thing.
I make the world a bargain: *I have something to show
you; if you don't stay in one place,
you'll only see whiffs*. I allow it admission
to my body. I say *breeze, work your touch
into my frays, everything else, away!*
The world is too much tonight. Its muchness
is enough to wring me dry. I can't help but watch
when no one is looking. Silly world, my eyes
are your magnets. I think the world wants me
to love it enough I don't need my hands
all over it. It wants me to watch a couple kiss
each other's sunspots, nuzzle into embrace,
then separate. I hope when Queen Elizabeth
married England, she was thinking
about fucking the world. The world won't tell me
what it wants, but I think it likes when stepping
from my car door, I quickly flash the pink
of my underwear. It did this undulation

in the leaves. It doesn't need party hat invitations.
I think I owe the world a thank you.
It didn't ask me to come here,
to sit at this bar top & buy myself a drink,
& yet I still came.

On Reserve

When I move through night, I carry
a seashell in my pocket. It is good

to have a delicate thing to protect.
It is like dawn brushing night

away in bluish streaks but much lighter.
If you try to photograph it, the blue

looks pale & sickly & suddenly
it's morning. There is some scheme bigger

than I'll ever reach that decides if I dance
tonight. A spiraled whale's bone

hangs from my neck on thick, black string;
it symbolizes infinity, but I won't ask it

to stand for that. Our world is not a top,
yet I believe in its spins. Sometimes

I spin much faster than the world.
I wear billowy dresses so the world

can see. Unless the gifts you gifted
are smaller than an envelope,

I don't have them. It's a space I gave myself
with limits at a time when I needed

limits. Our city is sliced
with train tracks. We call downtown

the center, but it's just a phrase
we use to feel cradled in canopies

of noisy lights. There are no archives
for people like us. If I meet you here,

I'll have no method to separate you
from any given walker. I can't tell you how

to get here—it would be
too risky—but you'll get there.

Everywhere & All at Once

Daytime & nighttime together, a quiet
dusk stroke, a pink so precise it tastes grapefruit.
I was thick with rhythm at the laundromat,
shaking quarters in time with the dryers' tumbling,
wandering. Out the broad windows, the sky,
now open & porous: a whisking motion, a party
with no invitation. I couldn't be blamed for dancing
without music. I wouldn't be rewarded
for my own wilderness. It started everywhere
& all at once, the way animals might fall in love
or citizens move to riot. And when my body subsided,
the room hushed in its unruffling;
the sky still there, a fuchsia lipstick-kiss,
the tumbling less damp, but still heavy
in density. What would I need to give up
(suspense? the articulation of plans?) to dig up
into this sky of sweetness, this twilight-splayed
pattern—what would be my reward
to know hardness as softness with a different face?

Nightlife

The light moved in lines, soft & strung
along the dance floor, spiraling
in slow creaky turns like carnival rides.
The trouble is feeling the red inside
without forgetting it moved alone, solo
when I am & am not looking.
I was too swamped with watching
the feet light-lines brightened
to remember I had a body
that should be swaying,
twirling—anything beyond standing.
Like bubbling preceding boiling,
a thought about colors was taking shape:
maybe they had some liberty. And to use them
to speak for me (*I am blue, the day feels
gray*), I would need to give some care
in return. I thought it natural to begin with love,
& like most things, I couldn't choose
which option most right to love.
I had loved worlds of colors
but with so little consequence. The deep
navy like the night was all around,
so it seemed a place

logical to begin. And when I branded to it
like it could make me sharper
or stronger by doing so, it seemed a sticky floor
I could only rid by evading, so I stuck
& stuck & felt my navy-night
in the space between shapes
where we first learn reach. Cold & light
like breeze through a window screen,
it was pleasant, so we stayed. All was midnight
cool tonic where bodies move towards gift
with such little thought of gain.

IV

It's Twelve

Sleep is too dense, like losing
oneself in suburban sprawl. Falling
into it is like waiting for day

to find purpose. The city
reminds with too little being. It holds
no weight; the noises

it makes compare to other
noises. If we keep moving here
to there with so little

settling, few things will cling.
Tetherless is both frightening
& freeing; solid & liquid

weigh just the same.
Cars find speed outside the window.
If probability holds,

I've met hundreds
of believers—at least one is believing
me. Simplicity can't be

a thwart to invention.
Something must enhance from plain
devotion: the day

to a teacup, night to the saucer
sustaining it—staring still
without turning it underneath

or testing its volume.
The ceiling is shallow; it confines
a whole litany

of memory—how we keep loving
with such balance: just enough weight
for impression, just enough

room to flee. A single down feather
finds its flutter, & it's still
too early for sleep.

The Party as It's Ending

Some skies turn dark in shades so sly
we can't see their variations.
So few ever learn this skill
(reading time through light),
instead we think night manifests in the body:
ten, a floaty bobbing belly;
twelve, a fast frequent surge atop the heart.
Some spaces fill in certain spans of time:
this room was tiptop to the brim
as it had everbeen. It didn't help
that the walls held too many photos
& in bold bass-pulses nearly buckled
from the load. Every once & again,
a fevered dancer would jerk one crooked
with a loose limb. The room crouched
that 12-watt slight-darkness,
dimming movements into mystery:
a thumb's soft-stroke inside a palm,
skip-trip on a scrunched rug.

And when the night billowed down
& out, the room followed: first, the people
found their coats & each exit landed
like a streak of morning leaden
on the sky. Then, the music,
now with so few to cling to, drifted pulpy
to the ceiling. It mattered little:

us, few, left with energy in our eyes.
Even our fiercest cries for fervor
felt lull & slug in taut throats.

So these efforts rearranged into straightening:
every plate clean, every surface
scrubbed new, as if this repurposing
could bring back a gleam of evening.
Once the last wild frame was tilted right,
we turned from one another.
Had night's dim cover ever colored our eyes?
The room was as plain as it had everbeen.
Not a single scuff on a wall to prove
a body tried to extend its boundary.
Not one blotchy stain or overturned vase.
Hopefully some particle of night—
that levitating in the belly, the clang
of clanking glass—burrowed
in my person like a place to return to.

But everbeen is a relative term:
it contains only what we can remember.

Everending Night

Hours trickled as our shoes spun circles
off the porch's wooden beams. Still,
when the night sky fissured into pale light streaks
the way growth accumulates with no notice,
I was startled. And when it stayed this musty haze
for distances, we held our voices
in the bold tone of retirement; our bodies
sloping towards the deck's exit.

And since we weren't granted our usual rites
of leaving or being left—wrapping scarves
about our necks or blankets in our bed,
there was no need to recollect.
The sky wasn't static like a photograph;
it replenished itself in sips: fresh grazes
on new rifts. This lingering became a lodging;
this lodging, a state of being. A time still near us,
petty parts slivered from me as we talked,
like clapping dry clay from hands: *here,*
it is clean again. But in the everending night,
these flakes find dwelling. Actions long memory,
to cabin somewhere cool & lasting
even if far flung from the self.

I didn't realize then with layers of light
interrupting night, my hands
in my pockets, *oh what time, the time,*

but I may never love what lacks potential
for farewell. I couldn't crumple inside a thing
the way the faithful do. Yet I trusted
that sky would break way to day.
Because I want to believe in rhythm,
because it's rendered in the stars, because
I still haven't found a fitting place to receive you.

A Light

Every meadow is a lesson:

                                  wide span;

the grasses' stretch doesn't reach anywhere,

just winds back in & touches itself.

The closest person I love is sixty miles away.

To be wrapped in familiar arms,

I would wait an hour—

                        if they sped to me.

I construct these little formulas

to articulate my lonely.

                 How long

I've wanted my own empty dryer drum.

Now having it, I wear three outfits a day

to even fill it every so often.

                       When people

mistake their tears solely for beauty,

they've missed the center.

                  Astronauts tearing

at the size of the world;

how they can cover its whole-round

with a thumb.

             No one wants to be useless.

Not even the world.

            My lonely

will never know a lonely quite like its own.

It is a photograph it can't zoom out of.

The outermost I've seen the world
is from an airplane:

                       snow-dipped tips
of Rockies.

            My lonely was most of me
that morning.

            I won't call the person
sixty miles away.

            I'll love them
when their headlights sweep my windows,
but each inch moves
in minutes,

            & if I feel fuller before
their arrival, what will I explain?

There's a teensy moth in the house winging
over & around my vision.

                  Look how flighty
& close it is. It thinks

            I am a light.

If This Is a Clearing

Yet-tread grass,
woodland opening, sponge meadow,
door ajar in the center
of night.

If this is a clearing, can I capture it?
Like model ships, their intricate masts
encased in glass liter bottles;
build the vessel, then whistle form
to hold it.

Cling into me, clearing.
Shush-sway rudders your tongue.
Does your twitch long for extension?
to stay? does your absence feel the wind?
are you waveless?

My body is a fastened
clasp-latch thing. Can I be a broad pardon,
my own long glade?

And if I've mistaken this expanse,
if my eyes prove sour-watchers,
if this stretch is, in fact,

         a separation,

I see the trees on its edges move.
Let me better approach them.

The World Provides

I.

If I move one street south
it's like walking a city I've never been in.
The world provides such pockets to fall
in slight pleasure with. Like sleeping
in someone's favorite sweater, waking up
with its fine threads in my mouth.

2.

Once I watched someone serenely open
a letter's clean folds like whatever quiet lay inside
they were tasked to watch over.

3.

Is it possible to have pure empathy
for a cockroach, even those wedged
in drain grates? Or is thinking it *helpless*
mostly the self?

4.

The sun & a silver watch make a spot, light
& little, to dance-shimmer
round the room. Can we help but want reckless
love's image in this?

5.

The world provides plenty of points
to fix on: leaves leaving fossiled forms
in wet concrete, powdered sugar
pasted sweet to some love's cheek.

6.

As if when we go lost & away,
these flecks that held our attention
so utterly will stand as seal we were here.
The breeze is just the right fervor
to make shapes with our hair
against the sunken-sure sky.
Together, we make a den to revel in.

Hands Full

I did it with my hands. Sometimes one
outstretched before my breast; the other,
a *come hither*. I did it with calculation,
other times without knowing. I hid below

the staircase, cowered from the rain. I did it
with my heart the way people do things
with their mouths. I said the words precisely
three days late; not-listening-speaking—

I held it like a bookend to a book,
still pushing beside to feel its warmth. I did it
with my mind. Blueprint-perfect urges,
a pearl in its world of a shell. Once I left

when planned. Once I didn't leave
at all. We forgot there was never not
time before now. I crushed my hand to sleep,
finally felt my own creased palm.

It said life would be full, of what
who could say. Once I danced my own body,
pretended joints dashed intervals
up my arms. I did it with my hips,

with a hand tangled in hair. I did it & kept
doing it until the song finished & fullness
flattened smooth. Are the dark rooms we fill
for vitality of life or where it most needs

to decompress? I thought on the last image
I loved: a reflection of the sky
in a photo frame. We can hold this,
although briefly. Sometimes the drums

have to kick in. Sometimes the rain
has to start, then stop. Your life will be full
of something; that will have to be enough.
I muttered an honest nothing. I lied

about what I was thinking. I loved it
with all my caution. I thought on it until
it moved *just right*. The sky is framed;
the rose birds are bound to a peach sky.

I touched you the way music
grasps its rhythm. I couldn't not.
I did it with my hands.

Tonight

If it was going to start, it was going to be small:
a perfect helix curl in my hair;
foot taps along a steady melody.

If it would happen, it might as well happen
like patchwork or not at all.
Lights dimmed to the edge of non-existence

as I swiveled my chair. Not a typical
debate of lingering or leaving,
rather the hazards of diving

& sinking. It wasn't New York City
or L.A., but clusters of buildings scraped the dark;
their windows, tiny light-filled cardinals

patterning the night. When I picked diving,
I dove. If it was going to work,
it had to be barely perceptible:

my fingertips tracing water circles
on a wooden table, a glance
through strands of hair.

Someone turned a knob on speakers
the way stakes in movies rise alongside volume.
I wasn't the femme fatale.

I wasn't going to whisper life
into the lifeless. I wouldn't return what's lost
or forgotten, this night

or any. Like grains of sand found in old pockets,
we'll remember it simply & fondly,
a red sequin snapped free

of a favorite dress. If I was going to love
this cherry-topped thing, or me,
or anyone, it was going to take years,

but this is irrelevant: it was tonight.

Today I Find Myself

for V

as if a daisy in a sea of tattered leaves,
the crisp grass only the Texas sun
can green.
                    I think how marvelous,
how wonderful that I was inward or leaky
or longing—how glistered I am now;
                                        my eyes
like spangled-static.
                        Look at what electric
they cling to:
                    translucent gecko, sun-washed
flag—how the world taunts its own erasure!
I close them:
                    the yard is full of leaves rustling
or oceans raging.
                        I imagine bodies
a little-salty-little-wet, sand sticks
to skin;
            we move new in earth-caked limbs.
I want to find myself fresh daily:
                                        to spin
suddenly towards a mirror & meet myself,

then greet myself as if having never seen
myself.
       Maybe it's not a mirror, but a you
on the other side of it.
            Maybe you are a mirror:
velvet treble of your voice gauges
my reflection;
        your reach to me, a ruler
(how much ardor did the world
store up, tell me).
       Tell me
how your day was, did you see winter
on the walk to your car;
           did the heat cough
hazy through your vents
or did you drive blocks, blowing breath
into your palms?
       In my thoughts,
sometimes I feel your face
is your face:
        skin silken until it meets rough-patch
then flesh-mouth;
      other times,
you're a planetary blaze, a bundle
of swelter.
       I've asked for a little of your warmth.

I've driven all night to keep the engine
running;

          I've brought goods (pages, kinesthesis,
salt from the ocean) to barter
your affection.

            If I've already lost myself,
it was overflow that did it:

                 too much brimming
to stand at your door, display what I found
while I still cupped it
in my chest.

          I loosen at the seams:
look

      what good fluff we're made of.

Acknowledgments

Thank you to the editors of the following journals in which these poems first appeared, sometimes in slightly different forms:

Blue Earth Review: "A Cantaloupe"

Bodega: "The Beginning"

The Boiler: "It's Seven," "On Reserve," & "Everending Night"

Cimarron Review: "Everywhere & All at Once"

Day One: "The Expansion"

decomP: "Party Planning"

Denver Quarterly: "If This Is a Clearing"

Fugue: "Even in Disguise"

Glass: A Journal of Poetry: "The Heart That Loves Is Always Wrong"

Grist: "The Party," "If I Erase My Body," "The World Wants"

Gulf Coast: "Interior Music" (originally titled "Outside Rushing In")

JuxtaProse: "A Light"

Lumiere Review: "Today I Find Myself"

New South: "Hands Full"

Nine Mile Magazine: "To Better Describe It," "The World Will Not Meet You Here," "It's Nine," & "It's Twelve"

No Tokens: "We Want the World"

Quarter After Eight: "Singing"

The Rush: "Place Shape" & "Tonight"

Southern Indiana Review: "The Gold Door"

The final section of "Eleven Versions of Taking Off My Lover" references the painting *Patch of Grass* by Vincent van Gogh. For this painting, Van Gogh reused an old canvas, & a portrait was discovered underneath the landscape.

The base image for *Eveningful*'s collage cover is a watercolor color blot (Crimson) by Mary Gartside published in 1808 in *An Essay on a New Theory of Colours*, and on *Composition in General*. Additional color blot images appear as section markers throughout the collection; including Blue, Violet, Crimson, Green, & Orange. Gartside is the first recorded woman to publish a theory of color, & her color blots are noteworthy for their shift towards a more organic, fluid understanding of color. I'm grateful to art historian Alexandra Loske for her research & efforts to bring Gartside's work into the light.

All my gratitude to the people & places that made this work in this form possible:

To the Lightscatter Press board & Lisa Bickmore for your belief in this collection & your care in shaping it.

To Rick Barot—thank you for selecting this manuscript & crafting a lovely avenue into it.

To Elizabeth Fuller for your beautiful paintings in response to this work, for inspiring me to see the world of *Eveningful* anew.

To Texas State University & the L.D. & LaVerne Harrell Clark House for gifting me invaluable time & space to think & re-think these poems.

To Ben Seanor—thank you for your insight & friendship, for offering your eyes to these poems so carefully so often.

To my teachers who showed me what is possible—with words & for myself: Kathleen Peirce, thank you for your light & warmth; for seeing me & this work so clearly. Kelly Moffett, every poem is a spark of gratitude to you. Cecily Parks, thank you for your steady encouragement, kindness, & advice. John Alberti, Cyrus Cassells, John Cullick, Emily Detmer-Goebel, Daniel Lochman, & Debra Monroe—thank you.

To my fellow writers & friends who offered feedback, advice, & encouragement: Dan Barton, Claire Bowman, Meg Cass, Scott Fenton, Maggie Ilersich, Katelin Kelly, Reyes Ramirez, Sean Rose, Micah Ruelle, Vincent Scarpa, & all those who wrote alongside me in Texas & Kentucky.

& to Nick—for your light; for all our days & nights.

About the Poet

Jennifer Whalen (she/her) is a poet & educator from the Northern Kentucky/Cincinnati, Ohio area. She received her M.F.A. from Texas State University where upon graduation she served as writer-in-residence at the university's Clark House (2015-2016). She currently teaches English at the University of Illinois Springfield.

Eveningful is her first book of poems.

About the Press

When light encounters an object, it bends and scatters: as a form of energy, it passes through the air, then shifts and deflects in ways not entirely predictable. At Lightscatter Press, we seek to publish the work of writers whose writing diffracts as it meets the world, finding life and light in multiple forms.

Blue.

A

73